The Quest

What happened to me that day was the start of a quest to live a life with meaning and purpose. I realized I could no longer do the job as Director of Railroad Operations. When I graduated from college, I made a commitment to make people's jobs safer. I had reached a point where I wanted more, and I wanted to share it with everyone. It was time to be honest and admit I had been struggling as an employee, boss, spouse, and even as a Dad.

I wanted to be able to teach people how to live, not just how to keep them safe. I wanted so much more for myself and even more for other people. There was just one problem: I did not know how to go about doing it.

Throughout the past several years there was a local businessman who had been trying to get me to work for him. I had turned him down several times, even though the money was about the same. I had a good job and really liked the people with whom I was working; however, after this "Peak Experience" (the point in someone's life that changes them forever), I knew I was ready to do something different.

I started dreaming about what that was and had a hard time finding it. Instead I kept myself engaged by working long hours and claiming to be too busy to figure it all out. About four months later that same local businessman approached me again to see if I now wanted to work for him. This time he made me an offer I could not refuse. I clearly knew timing was everything, and it was my time. I agreed to take the position.

As I ventured down a new path, I was committed to finding the answers to some of my as well as other people's problems. In particular I sought the answer to this question: Why are some people more successful and happier than others? That was the start of an amazing and exciting journey: The journey to find out what drives businesses to be happy.

Matthew J Cowell

Chapter 1 - Communication

Big challenges are a part of growth. One of my toughest initial challenges was to figure out how this new workforce's communication differed from that of the old workforce. Technology, specifically, was a big concern. I needed to understand how it impacted workplace communication.

I learned

- Over the past ten years the amount of information thrown at us has increased a hundred fold.

- We are being marketed on average 30,000 times a day via email, billboards, Internet ads, etc.

- The average person looks at his/her phone 150 times a day.

- Women use over 20,000 words a day compared to men who use about one-half that amount.

- Emails, text messages, and instant messaging accounts for most formal communication.

- Email is the best personal organization system for other people's personal agendas.

- The amount of misunderstood information is causing chaos within organizations.

With the modern workforce in information overload, the key to successful communication is how well someone can take in information, process and filter it, and then communicate it to others.

Through research I discovered only one person could truly make a difference in an individual employee - the manager. Management has to make it his/her priority to make sure communication and workplace conditions are as attractive as possible and then create meaning and value within every job. The study of positive psychology suggests being involved in something larger than personal self creates a sense of meaning and well-being, an essential part of the experience of happiness.

It became clear the ultimate goal of management was to create value through labor of people working together for a common cause. To achieve a healthy, productive, and happy workplace you must

>   Provide clear goals.
>   Provide adequate feedback.
>   Provide a balance of skills *vs.* abilities.
>   Make employees feel connected.
>   Never devalue an employee's time.

The items listed above are vital to every employee's success. Most people are not being provided the information listed above. When these things do not occur in the workplace, other things start to happen with employees that are not optimal. The human mind is programmed to turn threats and unfinished business into failures, leaving us unfulfilled because we do not feel needed as we have nothing urgent to do. When that happens, the mind is left free to wander. It ultimately leads to progressive depression because we have no tasks to focus our attention. I learned from studying corporate patterns that most management training companies or programs failed to mention the human nervous system functions best when challenged or focused on a task. In other words, most of us feel the best about ourselves after a job well done.

What is happiness?

Happiness is not something that happens, but something towards each of us must work. As you go through this book, I will break

Calls in the wee hours of the morning are seldom good. I will never forget one night back in 2007, when I was awakened by my cell phone ringing at 6:04 A.M. I did not recognize the number.

The voice on the other end said something like this: *This is the answering service. We just got a report of a train vehicle fatality in your town. It occurred at approximately 5:57 A.M. when a southbound train hit a car by Mile Marker XYZ.*

I knew the location and sprung into action. I got dressed, grabbed my bag and headed out the door. As I made the long drive across town, I realized I had not even let my wife know I was leaving. It was a holiday and she was still in bed, taking advantage of a rare morning to sleep in.

When I arrived on the scene, I was the second person on site. I noticed the county sheriff was already there. I went up to him, introduced myself, and showed my credentials so he knew I had clearance to be there.

We began to explore the scene, immediately noticing a white compact car resting up against the engine of the train. Trying to disconnect the car from the train, the engineer had backed the train up, but it was a futile effort. Both the sheriff and I looked at the car, and he informed me there were no passengers in the automobile. This meant either the car was abandoned or someone had been thrown from it. We looked around and not seeing anyone right away, we started walking. After about 70 feet we noticed a lifeless body lying down the embankment of the tracks. We walked over to the body, assessed it and realized there were no signs of life.

The sheriff said she was dead, confirming what seemed most obvious. We rolled the body over, and I noticed something immediately – something that was not a normal occurrence for me. She did not have any scratches, cuts, or bruises on her face. If she was thrown from the vehicle, this did not make any sense. It certainly did not add up that she had no marks after connecting with a moving train.

My mind immediately went into a spiral which I still cannot explain to this day. Yes, in the past I had found body parts or remains, but that was not the case this time. In front of me was a perfectly normal human being. I started to take notes about her and noticed she was very petite and dressed for work. I just kept thinking she is going to get up, brush herself off, and then be on her way. Yet that did not happen.

I will admit I had to take a few minutes to think about what I saw. After that I proceeded to do my investigation of the accident. After a few minutes, the sheriff came and asked if I would help him. I nodded and followed him.

We arrived back at the spot where the deceased lady's body was. The sheriff directed the coroner to pull into a small driveway, blocking the body from the media who had started to arrive on the scene. The vehicle could not get close enough to the tracks, so we picked her up and carried her the 15 feet to the vehicle, placing her body in a black bag on the stretcher. I will never forget the sound of that zipper as it closed. At that very moment my life changed forever.

After accident investigations it was not uncommon for me to go into a funk for a few days, thinking about what I had seen and trying to make sure I had pieced all the information together properly. However, something about this lady's death really bothered me. For the next several days I walked around in a daze, having a hard time focusing.

down many different parts of what it takes to work happily, but first I want you to see the big picture of happiness.

In today's world we have so many different ways of communicating with each other. It is overwhelming how many times and ways we communicate. Since we have become a global society, we have stimuli coming at us from many different sources:

What is interesting to understand is the overstimulation in today's economy. We receive around 7,000 stimuli every day. Less than 200 years ago a person did not receive that much stimuli in a lifetime. The most important thing to ask yourself is this question: "Is the information coming at me *positive* or *negative*?" Being able to clearly define this is critical to understanding the relativity of happiness in your world.

The information we absorb is not overwhelming, but we must understand how the brain processes the information and how that affects us. The stimulus come into the brain from our five senses and then is received by the limbic part of the brain. From there the limbic part sends neurons to the prefrontal cortex of the brain, but only if we are in a calm state, which I will explain more about later.

The human brain is the most complex and powerful system in the world because we have a conscious and an unconscious part. Let us distinguish the difference between the two: The conscious part of the brain leads us to behaviors/thoughts and/or habits. We have to make conscious choices to exert energy into something to happen or change behaviors. All changes in the brain begin with the conscious mind (choice). The unconscious part of the brain takes in the information through our five senses. The most amazing part is that the unconscious part of the brain cannot distinguish between a truth and a lie.

Thus the first step in determining happiness is to find a way to tip the scale to make sure you are only allowing positive information into your mind. There will always be negative information being thrown at you, but you have to make sure you are inserting more positives than negatives. This begins with you.

The next phase of happiness is to understand we have three levels of time in which each person lives.

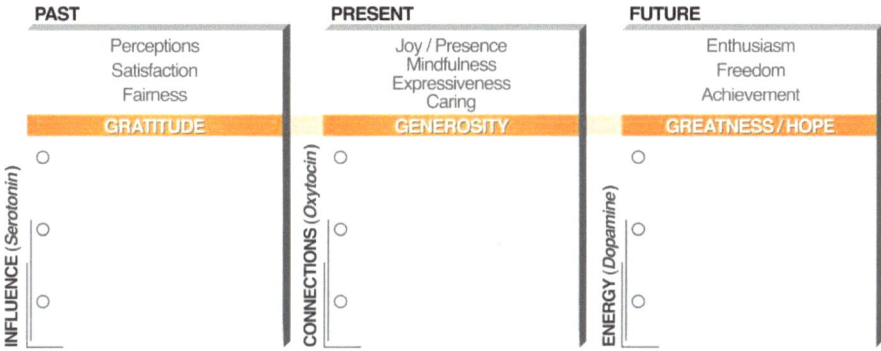

The first element of happiness is to understand our past and be okay with who we are. The experiences you have had in life are what make up who you are today. Good or bad -- this is who you are; you cannot change these experiences. Allow yourself to be grateful for all of those experiences because you would not be here today if you did not have them. Be thankful life has given you the opportunity to mold and shape yourself.

The most powerful element we have is gratitude. When you understand the powers of gratitude in yourself, the process of being happy begins. This will allow you to leave the first time zone, your past. When you show and share your gratitude for your past with others and demonstrate gratitude towards others, you begin to speed up the journey of happiness.

The second element of happiness is to understand present time, which means understanding where you currently are and expressing the joy of gratitude for that. You may not be content with the exact space you are in your life, but wanting to show generosity and appreciation for where you are is the second element of happiness. Stop and enjoy where you are, and be thankful for what you have and for the experiences you have had.

The third time element is the future. We must believe tomorrow or some other future time will be better than today. If we live in the past or present, we are not thinking towards making ourselves or things better. That is being content. There is nothing wrong with contentment, but the brain is always seeking a new challenge or opportunity. If we always stay the same, the brain is not balanced. The right side wants to be pushed to learn, grow and find new and better ways of doing things.

We have to understand how powerful this time element is in being happy. The future is about hope or greatness. Hope is the ability to aspire to do things you want in order to make yourself great. This is VITALLY important because in addition to gratitude, the most important element for happiness is the ability for individuals to have control. Control is critical in understanding happiness. In workplace happiness the less control someone has in his/her job the less likely he/she is to stay or be engaged in the job. For the past twenty-five years the number one reason people leave their job (self-reported up to a year later) is they do not feel valued or appreciated, meaning they did not feel as if they were in control of what they could accomplish while in the previous job. Consequently, the ability to grow and create a better work environment through goals or create hope to make things better was not present, so employees did not feel connected to the organization.

The opposite of happiness is stress. Stress is caused by the brain releasing cortisol into the body. Cortisol then attacks the muscles making them tense, raises blood pressure, and does many other things which I will explain in later chapters. Happiness is more than something that just happens to us. Happiness at work is even harder to achieve. It is a conscious choice. In order to create a happy workplace culture, you must make choices. If you only get one takeaway from this book, implement the process of gratitude into every meeting or day. This will make a difference in sales, retention, and overall performance of your organization.

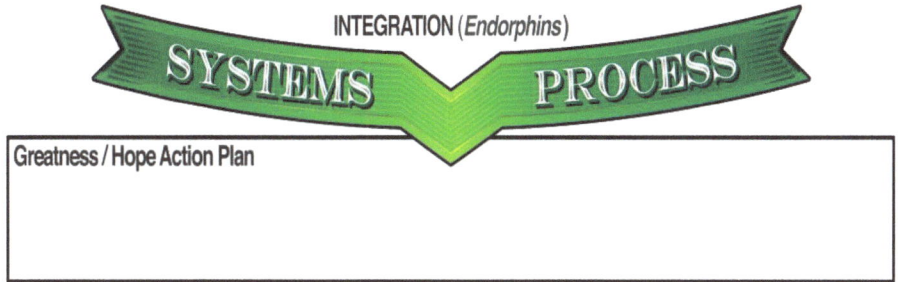

What Is a Happy Organization?

A happy organization is one in which the goal(s) is clearly defined, and management creates a culture of creating value through engaging its people to produce a positive environment along with a high level of accountability. All employees feel connected to the organization and are willing to give above the average norm.

Finding Happy People and Organizations

My quest to find happy people and organizations has been difficult, but when you teach business owners how to implement the High Achievers Framework, you will get amazing results. I have lived it, and I see it with the people I work with every day.

Business organizations whose employees are happy are more productive and have higher morale and lower turnover. Consequently, this makes it very relevant and important for managers to understand what makes people happy and implement that knowledge as effectively as possible.

Contrary to what most of us believe, happiness does not just happen or exist within us without some sort of action toward being so. It is something we make happen, and it occurs when we do our best. Feeling fulfilled when we live up to our potential is what motivates differentiation and leads to evolution.

People are designed to work; however, most jobs are not built for people to have clear goals. Even fewer jobs have goals which link the individual to the organizational goals. Yes, I had many questions and needed to find a way to get the sensible answers and lead to my quest.

Chapter 2 – The High Achievers Framework

This framework was developed to clearly identify how we can design our companies and incorporate the happy chemicals into a system that is easy for others to follow. I wanted to make sure any program I designed was able to fall into this system, and I could explain exactly what was going on and why. I wanted to make sure that every process, system, or training was meeting a purpose under our framework.

Energy: When applied properly, energy that is positive and focused will move projects and people to new heights. However, that energy has to start with you. Others thrive from what the power plant produces, and so it is with the leaders and organizations of today. With clear mission, vision, and goals there is no stopping you or the organization.

Connections: Once an individual is able to harness that energy and form good solid connections with those he/she leads or works with, true culture begins developing. As a leader linking an employee's job/role with the success of the organization's goals and strategies truly shows employees are making a difference. In turn this drives them to top performance. You must be well connected in the same manner and represent what you wish to have happen.

Influence: When a leader applies positive energy to the connections he/she has in the workplace and then learns the true art of influence, organizational success is right around the corner. A true leader realizes the days of power leadership are gone, and for success to happen today it is all about influence leadership.

Integration: The final step before great results can be achieved throughout the organization is integration. When you combine positive energy, connections, and influential leadership with efficient systems and processes, you achieve the High Achievers Culture in your workplace.

Let us take a look at this from an organization's point of view:

Company Mission along with Values and Goals = **Energy**.

Organizational Purpose which lets everyone know why the company exists and the historical view of who it is today = **Connection.**

Clearly Defined Accountability is who is responsible for reporting to whom within the organizational structure = **Influence.**

Efficient Systems and Processes are procedures with everyone working together for a common goal = **Integration.**

Management's job is to connect the organizational goals to individual employee's job. Most leaders do not tie the two together, but it is essential to do so.

We have identified the tasks under each of the four areas of our leadership model and listed out how each one is linked to the organization. Each leader or manager should be held responsible for making sure every employee understands the following:

Energy:

Energy is the extent to which an organization or team or business unit, depending on your responsibility, has mobilized this kind of emotion. It is cognitive and has potential for the goals of a business or work unit team to have the same goal you have. Organizational energy means looking at the emotions such as passion, excitement, or cognition of its people. We need to ask the following questions:

- How alert is the organization?
- How awake is the organization?
- Is the organization looking for opportunities and behavior changes?
- Is the organization using effort and engagement to fuel it and strive for energy?

Energy is the state of your human resources - the forces you have. How much are you activating your people? Activating your people is involving them in decision-making processes, making them see and reach their goals. Later you will learn how energy releases dopamine in the brain, making you want to work towards a goal. Setting goals is the biggest trigger of releasing dopamine because it looks to the future/hope.

We use the High Achievers Business Analysis™ survey to look at four different levels of energy:

- Productive Energy
- Conservative Energy
- Inertia Energy
- Corrosive Energy

Productive Energy is the level of intensity people are actually engaged in within the organization. Engaged employees are plugged in and feel as though they are part of the team or culture. They feel valued and appreciated. These highly alert organizations have a lot of effort behind their initiatives.

Conservative Energy includes organizations that are highly satisfied with what they are doing. These organizations are not really questioning the status quo of their processes and strategies. They are somewhat at ease, changing incrementally, but not questioning whether this is actually what they should do in the future.

Inertia Energy are organizations or teams who are detached from the organization. They are doing nine-to-five but no more, designated, and slightly frustrated. So often organizations or teams that go through a lot of change think they are not able to succeed. They believe they are not able to make a difference, and with too much change they become burned out.

Corrosive Energy is highly intense people working inside the organization for all the wrong reasons. Typical indictors are things such as a high level of conflict, mutual betrayal, always against the agenda of the organization, and individuals promoting only their ideas and agenda.

Energy:

- Understand the overall job of the employee and how it relates to the organization.

- Make sure the employee understands the mission and vision of the organization and help him/her realize he/she is connected to something bigger than himself/herself.

- Include the employee in setting team goals as well as his/her own personal goals.

- Make sure leaders and employees frequently communicate the organizational goals.

- Provide frequent (weekly) progress meetings as to how the employees are doing.

- Develop performance measures and business unit Key Performance Indicators (KPIs) to let the employees know if they are winning or losing at their job.

- Provide a purpose-driven schedule.

- Make sure employees understand the core values of the organization and hold them accountable.

- Include current employees in the hiring of new employees.

- Evaluate performance frequently.

Connection:

High-quality connection is the term we use to designate short-term, dynamic, positive interactions at work. The positivity of high-quality connection is known by how you feel for persons involved, what they do, and the beneficial outcomes produced. The feeling of a high-quality connection can be experienced as the uplift felt when encountering someone who expresses genuine concern for how you are doing after a grueling meeting or work shift.

The foundation for a high-quality connection is based on three areas: cognitive, emotional, and behavioral mechanisms which explain how to determine the level of connection. We define work connections as the dynamic energy existing between two people at work when there is some interaction involving mutual awareness.

First, we assume humans are intrinsically social and have a need to belong. Second, while we interact with each other, the connections are dynamic and change as individuals alter how they feel, think, and behave. Third, we know the work of organizations is performed through social processes, and connections are key elements for understanding how work is accomplished. Fourth, we assume connections vary in quality. Differences in quality reflect variance in how healthy and well-functioning the relationship is at a particular point in time.

One differentiation is the positivity of the people involved and the emotional experience of each individual in the connection. The second impacts the connection that enhances the potentiality and responsiveness of the connection. Positive experiences impact the vitality of feelings in the connection. People who have high-quality connections feel positive stimulus and a heightened sense of positive energy. Being positive denotes a sense of feeling known and loved or being respected and cared for in connection. This allows for both people to feel movement in the connection and should be noted it also exposes vulnerability and responsiveness when full participation is experienced.

Connectivity describes a connections level of openness to new ideas and influences. High-quality connections also facilitate individual's recovery and adaption when employees are suffering from loss or illness thus undergoing transitions in their careers or jobs. High-quality connections are important as a means by which people develop and grow, and they are also associated with greater levels of psychological safety and trust. Higher levels of interpersonal trust can enhance cooperation and trustworthiness.

Cognitive emotions highlight how conscious and unconscious thought processes predispose people to building high-quality connections. Emotional actions point out how feelings open people up to connection and are shared between people in ways that build high-quality connections. Behavioral actions determine how the two parties interact and share ideas and concerns.

Positive emotions broaden our thinking and help build durable, social resources. Gratitude, or thankfulness, occurs when an individual perceives that someone intentionally provides something valuable to another person. Feeling grateful towards others boosts attention to the positive qualities of both parties. It should also be noted that when positive emotions are shared, the person receiving the emotions unconsciously mirrors the emotions of the other person. In Chapter 4, "Happy Chemicals of the Brain," you will learn how connections are connected to releasing oxytocin, the brain /body's natural connection chemical.

Connection:

- Explain the overall organizational purpose and how each employee's job relates to build a connection.

- Include employees in the hiring process and allow them to help determine who is a good fit for the organization thus building a connection and trust.

- Be transparent and share things with your employees.

- Build an atmosphere in which employees can have open communications, but do not allow talking behind others' backs.

- Focus on developing employees helps connect people within the organization.

- Push employees in a positive direction in relation to job skills vs. knowledge.

- Understand team members' communication styles.

- Focus on internal customer service as much as external customer service.

- Teach people to develop and take risks.

- Disseminate information to all employees, not just a select few.

- Motivate and create a sense of teamwork through teambuilding and working through issues.

Influence:

As organizations become increasingly matrixes and global, the ability to influence others has become a must have for leaders. When working across functions and geographies, leaders are often expected to produce results through people over whom they have no direct authority. Influence is turning your agenda into theirs by gaining the commitment of others rather than forcing compliance.

Influence leaders must become more agile in their interpersonal relationships. They want to employ the full range of influencing others' behaviors which will enable them to project a new, more powerful image. They need to learn how to measure key colleagues (potential partners, fence sitters, and adversaries) and develop strategies for positioning their ideas and plans for maximum acceptance by each group.

Influence is about self-awareness and the degree to which leaders are viewed as a powerful, influential leading force in their organization. This is accomplished by learning communication techniques for modifying or changing their image and becoming a stronger force without a commanding tone. Influence is also about understanding and navigating organizational politics or forces. Developing important degrees of cooperation from key colleagues is essential. Leaders need to develop an influence plan that enables them to achieve results from across their organization. You will learn in Chapter 4, "Happy Chemicals of the Brain," how influence is related to releasing serotonin, the brain's natural elevating mood drug.

Influence:

- Empower workers to complete tasks and hold them accountable.
- Develop systems for complete accountability (See <u>The High Performance Business Model</u>).
- Have public-organizational charts with decision-level responsibilities identified.
- Build and work continually on restoring/maintaining trust.
- Make decisions based on the good of the organization, not just a select few.
- Learn how to effectively delegate (See our Delegation Navigator™).
- Remove barriers to success.
- Identify and reward positive behaviors.
- Include the group in scheduling.
- Realize customer service is not a one-size-fits-all model.
- Conduct honest, open performance evaluations.
- Make sure leaders are conducting their accountability checkups at the time and date committed.

Integration:

Integration is an extremely analytical, process-result oriented way of making decisions. Integration is about creating a culture which builds a direct, open and honest communication channel for all employees.

Integration is about developing processes and systems that set the climate for performance of the total organization in terms of expectations of individuals, departments, etc. Systems such as:

- Distribution Systems
- Long-term strategic issues
- Critical Mass
- Financial Integration
- Staff Integration/Human Resources
- Company changes
- Decision-making authority
- Clarification of roles/responsibilities
- Revenue/cost issues
- Value Systems

It would be foolish to establish a one-size-fits-all system for a company. It just does not work that way in today's workplace. The workplace of today wants total accountability that strives to keep employees informed in all areas of the business. Organizations need to be transparent in their actions and beliefs.

These five steps are musts when understanding integration:

- Have a clear, realistic shared vision.
- Understand the differences between employees and management.

- Know the people - organizations need to understand their fears and concerns.

- Define and implement the processes and tools.

- Engage, Engage, and Engage the workers.

Management needs to perform due diligence when communicating issues to employees. Employees will find out information about the organization before management is prepared to share if you do not have a communication plan. Do not lie to your employees, but when you can, share any information with them. It is imperative you do this. Holding back information only decreases the levels of integration within an organization and impacts employee loyalty and trust. You will learn in Chapter 4, "Happy Chemical of the Brain," how integration releases endorphins, the brain's natural feel-good chemical. Endorphins also kick in the closer we get to a goal.

Integration:

- Have clearly defined processes.

- Tie meetings to goals/objectives.

- Monitor and communicate the budget.

- Communicate and track Business Unit KPIs.

- Address issues in timely manner.

- Update processes and accountability as needed.

- Support ongoing training both personally and professionally.

- Empower others to cross training.

- Ensure reports are written correctly, and information is communicated to all parties.

- Organize work flow.
- Have clear accountability.
- Follow through.

When all steps of the High Achievers Framework are working together within an organization, you are laying the foundation to establish a High Achievers Culture. Whether it is communication skills, conflict resolution, leadership abilities or everyday decisions, they all have one thing in common: the human brain.

Chapter 3 – Understanding the Human Brain

The human brain has two sides and three dimensions. It has a left and right hemisphere, but it is more complicated than that. From the outside looking in, the left and right side of the brain look similar; however, they function very differently.

From a non-medical point of view, the left and right cerebral hemispheres look similar. Functionally, the left hemisphere involves speech and language, reasoning and analysis, and certain communicating actions which are based mainly on the left side in most people. Since nerve fibers cross from left-to-right at the base of the brain, this dominant left side receives sensory information from and sends messages to muscles in the right side of the body, including the right hand. The right hemisphere is more concerned with sensory inputs, auditory and visual awareness, creative abilities, and spatial awareness.

Left Hemisphere of the Brain

The left side of your brain makes your life very livable. It remembers how to drive to work each day, what side of the road to drive on, and which is the left and right leg as you put on your pants. Your left hemisphere loves linear, linguistic, logical, and literal communication. Also acting as a list maker, the left loves to label things. It specializes in reasoning, using chains of logic, and cause-effect relationships. It is very easy to spot it at work in a small child when they start asking, "Why? Why? Why?"

Right Hemisphere of the Brain

The right side of your brain is focused on creativity and emotions; it does not like change. This hemisphere is more directly connected to the subcortical areas of the brain. Information flows from the body to brainstem to limbic areas to the right cortex, somewhat disengaging the left hemisphere from these raw subcortical sources, physical sensations, brainstem-survival reactions, and our limbic feelings and attachments.

For example, cross your arms. Now cross them the other way. It does not feel right, does it? That is because the right side is telling the left side to "STOP." It does not like to do things that do not feel right. Another example is New Year's resolutions. Have you ever made one and not kept it? It is part willpower, but again you have the right side telling the left side that whatever you are trying to do is not normal. It does not feel right, so you need to stop. That is also why losing weight or quitting smoking is so difficult.

The Subconscious

The right hemisphere also is responsible for the subconscious part of the brain. It is important to understand the subconscious part of the brain is one of the most powerful parts because it allows us to think if things are possible or not. The only problem with the subconscious part of the brain is it cannot distinguish between a truth and a lie. Let me explain how I demonstrate this in my workshops:

> I call two people up to the front of the room. I introduce both of them to the class and ask if either of them has any neck or back injuries.
>
> I pick one of the subjects and ask him/her to raise his/her arms straight out in front of himself/herself. I then take my hands and show them to the class and the participants. I tell the participant with the outstretched arms to resist me with all the force he/she has when I try to push his/her arms down. Then I try to push his/her arms down.
>
> Next, I have the second participant stand in front of the first participant. They stand facing each other and about a foot apart. I instruct the second participant to do the following:

- Make up as many negative and false things about this person as possible.

- Tell these things for 30 seconds, getting as personal as possible.

After 30 seconds I have the first participant hold his/her arms out again. I then stick the palms of my hands on his/her wrists and inform he/she to not allow me to push down on his/her arms.

Without fail 99% of the first participants are not able to keep telling himself/herself that he/she is good enough or strong enough to keep me from pushing his/her arms down. I usually ask him/her to try several times just to prove the point.

When I ask the group why this happens, they are not sure. I explain the subconscious part of the brain cannot distinguish between a truth and a lie. It really does not matter what the issue or the subject is. If something is said repeatedly, the human brain starts to believe it.

I am particularly worried about our youth in this respect. Where do people go for positive information? The typical preschool-age child hears negative comments on the average of 422 times a day. We know from research it takes about seven positive comments to overcome one negative thought. Where do people go to hear positive information?

Unconscious Emotion

We have evolved a conscious emotional system, but we retain the primitive, automatic responses at the heart of emotion. A frightening sight or sound, for example, registers in the amygdala before we are even conscious of it. While the sensory information is sent to the cortex to be made conscious, the amygdala sends messages to the hypothalamus, which triggers changes readying the body for flight, fight, or appeasement. This quick, dirty route allows us to take instant action to save ourselves. When we startle at a loud noise and then relax after realizing it was harmless, we are experiencing both stages – unconscious reaction and conscious response.

The Creative Process

Our brains are continuously bombarded with stimuli, most of which are ignored. This shutting out ensures we use the most relevant information to guide our thoughts. Opening our minds to new information will initiate the creative process. This happens when the brain relaxes from sharp attentiveness produced by gamma waves into idling, which is characterized by slow, relaxed alpha waves. In this mode stimuli that might otherwise be ignored enter awareness and resonate with memories, generating new thoughts and ideas that may be both novel and useful.

Let us try to see how much of your creative mind you can access: Take both of your hands and place them in front of you. Hold them facing each other as in prayer but do not put them together or let them touch. Now start circling your right hand in a clockwise motion. Take your left hand and start circling in a counter-clockwise motion. Keep trying until you get this. This can be easy for those who allow clear access into the right side of their brain.

The Limbic System

The limbic system is deeply rooted inside the middle of the brain. It is crucial for forming relationships and becoming emotionally attached to one another. It is involved in instinctive behaviors, deep-seated emotions, and basic impulses such as sex, anger, pleasure, and general survival. It also forms a link between centers of higher consciousness in the cerebral cortex and the brainstem, regulating the body's systems.

The limbic system manages neurochemicals such as amygdala. It also directs the hippocampus, a seahorse-shaped cluster of neurons functioning as a master-puzzle-piece assembler linking together wide-separated areas of the brain. This integration of neural firing patterns converts our moment-to-moment experiences into memories.

You need both the cortex and the limbic system to make sense of the world. Your cortex sees the world as a chaos of detail until your limbic system labels things as good or bad for you. More importantly, your cortex cannot produce happy chemicals; this comes from your limbic system. Your cortex and limbic system are literally not on speaking terms because the limbic system cannot process language. When you talk to yourself, it is all in your cortex. The limbic system never communicates in words why it is spurting a happy or unhappy chemical.

Chapter 4 - Happy Chemicals of the Brain

It is imperative to understand the brain in order to see why we as humans do the things we do. In order to change behaviors we must first determine how the brain responds to being rewarded with reaching a goal.

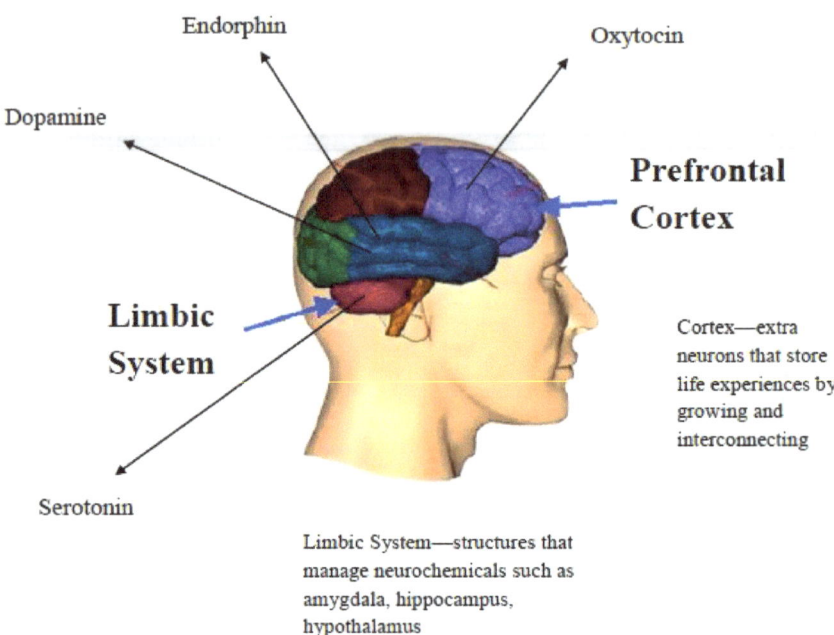

Happy Chemicals

In an effort to understand the brain better in order to learn how to lower cortisol, I found out the brain produces four chemicals that make us happy. *"Well, if that is true, why would we not design our businesses around making people happy?"* I thought. Understanding these four happy chemicals and the effect they have on a person is an important wealth of information for making your employees happy.

The feeling we call happiness derives from four special brain chemicals: dopamine, oxytocin, serotonin, and endorphin. The brain releases these happy chemicals when it sees something good. These chemicals are ready to release again when the next good thing crosses your path.

Each happy chemical triggers a different good feeling. Dopamine produces the joy of finding what you seek – the "Eureka! I got it!" feeling. Oxytocin produces the feeling of being safe with others – bonding. Serotonin produces the feeling of being respected by others – pride. Endorphin produces the oblivious state that masks pain- euphoria.

Happy chemicals are controlled by tiny brain structures all mammals have in common: hippocampus, amygdala, pituitary, hypothalamus, and other parts collectively known as the limbic system. In humans the limbic system is surrounded by a huge cortex where interconnecting neurons store life experiences. These two different brain systems are always working together, trying to keep you and your DNA alive. Your cortex looks for patterns that match patterns stored in the past. Your limbic system releases neurochemicals which tell your body, "This is good for you; go for it." or "This is bad for you; avoid it." Your body does not always act on these messages because your cortex can override them. Then, your limbic system tries again.

The cortex is good at avoiding bad feelings. We avoid hunger and chill by planting food and stocking fuel. However, unhappy chemicals remain no matter how well we meet our needs. As soon as we are fed and warm, our brain scans for other things that can hurt us. Our survival is threatened as long as we are alive, and our brain never stops looking for these threats.

Unhappy chemicals make us feel bad because that is how they work. Cortisol produces bad feelings. Your response to cortisol depends on what it is paired with such as low blood sugar, the sense of a near predator, social exclusion, or a myriad of other danger signals. When cortisol flows, it links the brain's active neurons allowing us to recognize those danger cues in the future.

When you feel a cortisol alert, it is like a flowing electrical current. Your brain begins looking for a way to make that feeling stop. The electricity in the brain finds the path of least resistance. Electricity does not flow easily along neurons that have never been activated. Your brain likes your old circuits even when they lead you astray. That is because electricity zipping down a well-worn pathway gives you the feeling of knowing what is going on. The bad feeling of resisting a habit eases once a new habit is formed. Then the neurons turn off, so they are ready to spurt again when something good crosses your path.

Dopamine

Dopamine is the body's natural chemical for finding the joy of discovering what you seek. This can be very easily explained by anyone playing any game on their Facebook or iPad. For example, the game Candy Crush has been designed to allow you to be rewarded by earning points for matching like candies and colors. The objects glow, disappear, and you earn points. More candies and colors are added to the screen. Why is this important? Because when you identify two like candies, you get a dopamine release. "I did it!" the brain tells the body. It feels so good the brain looks for ways to trigger the feeling again. What is important to notice is when you are playing a game such as this, you are getting smaller releases of dopamine. More importantly, you get a sense of "Wow!" which meets your needs. The dopamine surge connects all the neurons active in the brain at that moment. Gaming eliminates survival threats from the brain's perspective. The next time you feel bad, scoring points in a computer game is one way your brain knows to feel good. I am not advocating gaming your day away, but it is a highly effective way to get the boost of energy and happiness you may need.

Bigger goals require more dopamine, increasing the great feelings even further. Since dopamine releases energy into our body, it gives us a feeling of more energy. Many people get addicted to having this feeling in a crisis, and in time they become addicted to dopamine since it is associated with a rush and excitement.

When dopamine floods the prefrontal cortex, the executive center of your brain, your ability to focus and concentrate increases. When dopamine levels drop, the frontal lobes no longer do their job properly. Speech and thought are guided to a lesser degree, and your mind cannot plan as it should, making you lose track of your goals. In other words, exercise tightens your mental focus as well as your muscles. The more active you are, the more dopamine receptors are present. An obese, sedentary person actually has fewer dopamine receptors, and therefore, more trouble concentrating.

Brain scientists tell us mental energy comes from two sources: a high purpose in life and the right kind of fuel. The happy chemical does double duty. It creates a good feeling by unleashing energy, and it stores information that can lead you to the good feeling again.

Making Decisions

Intelligence is largely the ability to make sensible decisions which involves calculating pros and cons. First, the brain assesses the goal value, the reward expected as a result of the decision. Next, it calculates the decision value, the net outcome or the reward minus the cost. Finally, the brain makes a prediction of how likely it is the decision will deliver the reward envisaged. This can be compared with the actual outcome. The more complex the problem, the more the frontal area of the brain is involved.

In brain terms this would involve surges in the release of the chemical messenger dopamine which plays a central role in drive and reward. All addictive behavior, from gambling to the use of drugs such as cocaine and alcohol, involves activation of the dopamine systems. The rural areas initiating reward seem to overwhelm the prefrontal areas that regulate our more complex behaviors. Instead of being able to choose our actions, the drug chooses them for us. The reward circuit takes over, and our conscious cortical mind becomes a slave to the addictive drive.

When a dopamine spurt ends, it may feel as though something is wrong, but dopamine is supposed to rise and fall. Imagine your ancestor finding a river full of fish. He is very excited as he runs back to tell his clan about it. Dopamine creates the energy to run back and the memory to find the spot again. Serotonin might surge when he thinks of the respect he will get from his tribe, and oxytocin might spurt when he thinks of the shared pleasure of feasting. However, his dopamine will dip unless he finds more fish. When dopamine dips, your unhappy chemicals get your attention. You get that "Do something!" feeling causing you to decide what to do.

Oxytocin

Oxytocin is the reason I noticed the happy chemicals. I was in search of the natural body's response to lower cortisol levels and found the antidote called oxytocin, an anxiety reducer. This natural chemical is the body's way of lowering cortisol levels. I began to work with my local family doctors and found it is very common for them to just prescribe some sort of anxiety medicine instead of teaching patients how to lower cortisol. This really frustrated me as it seems society today just wants a quick fix.

When I first started researching and talking about oxytocin, most women knew about it. When a woman gives birth, her oxytocin level surges. Oxytocin also spikes in the newborn's brain, making it so a young child clings to his/her mother long before he/she comprehends that he/she is no longer connected. This sensation feels good to both the giver and the receiver.

Oxytocin produces a pleasurable feeling that promotes bonding. Just as the closely related hormone vasopressin, oxytocin helps the processing of social cues involved in the recognition of individuals and may play a role in placing a somewhat addictive effect such as dopamine. This may explain why people feel anguish at being separated from loved ones for any length of time. They miss the oxytocin rush involved in being with them.

Oxytocin is stimulated by touch and social trust. In animals touch and trust go together. In humans oxytocin is stimulated by everything from holding hands to feeling supported to orgasm. Holding hands stimulates a small amount of oxytocin, but when repeated over time, as in the case of elderly couples, it builds up a circuit that easily triggers social trust. Sex triggers a lot of oxytocin at once yielding lots of social trust for a very short time.

The release of oxytocin is critical because it puts the brakes on stress. When we have real connections with people, we show affection and emotional support. When friendships begin, this stimulates the oxytocin within us. How do we create a workplace where "Everybody knows your name," and we feel included, trusted, and safe?

Oxytocin may be released by

- Hugs (Non-sexual)
- A sense of belonging
- Connections
- Giving of yourself

Social media creates the need for us to comment on on-line forums. This is why Facebook, Twitter, Pinterest, Vine and Instagram are so popular. These things feel good because social trust stimulates oxytocin. That is why the brain is always looking for a chance to get more of that oxytocin feeling.

The brains of people who live constantly in the urgency mode are bathed in adrenaline and cortisol, the hormones that jolt you awake and keep you alert. Stressed-out folks may have elevated cortisol levels all day long. When your cortisol level is high, your body is stuck in the fight-or-flight mode: Veins and arteries are constricted, and blood pressure spikes. Chronically high cortisol levels can lead to a host of physical illness. You become negative, anxious, and unproductive.

Serotonin

Antidepressants such as Prozac are known for raising serotonin levels in the brain. They make you feel good and raise your mood. That is why family doctors are prescribing these pills without hesitation. However, that has resulted in merely masking the symptoms of release cortisol has. Why is serotonin so important?

Serotonin is stimulated by the status or aspect of love – the pride of associating with a person of a certain stature. It feels so good that people tend to seek it again and again. Getting respect feels good because it triggers serotonin. The good feeling motivates you to seek more respect, and that promotes survival.

I began noticing a trend: When you give people more trust and respect and show you value them as an individual, serotonin levels rise. This is something that can be taken to the workplace and used to make organizations happier and more prosperous.

As I dug into more aspects of serotonin, I found the brain is always trying to find ways to get more serotonin without losing oxytocin or increasing cortisol. For example, if your comment in a meeting gets respect, that feels good. Each time you receive respect, your brain links that and helps you figure out how to get more. Each time you lose respect, your brain links that and helps you avoid losing it in the future.

It reiterated a point I had noticed: The old style of management, which focuses on individuals having different levels of status or positions of power, really makes people feel less valued. I needed to find a way to get organizations to understand it was not in their best interests to exploit serotonin disappointment.

Serotonin inevitably dips because you cannot get increasing respect every moment of your life. When it dips, you might get the feeling that something is wrong with the world. The ups and downs of serotonin promote survival by balancing energy expenditure with food intake.

WORD OF CAUTION: Many people protect themselves from serotonin disappointment by saying they do not care about status. This is a justification you should strive to remove from your thought patterns.

Endorphins

The only thing I knew about endorphins was when you exercise, you release endorphins. That meant I associated them with pain. Endorphins are stimulated by physical pain. Even crying can stimulate endorphins.

Endorphin is called the body's natural morphine. The opposite is true: Morphine is an artificial endorphin. Street drugs such as opium or derivatives of opium such as heroin make you high because they trick the body into feeling as though you are producing natural endorphins which give you euphoria.

Euphoria is often used to describe the endorphin feeling, but this neurochemical did not evolve for good times. Physical pain is what triggers endorphins. Endorphins mask pain for a short time which promotes survival by giving an injured mammal a chance to reach safety.

Runner's high is the well-known endorphin experience, but a regular daily run does not make you high. You have to push beyond your capacity to the point of distressing your body to get that good feeling. This is not necessarily a good way to promote survival. Endorphins do not motivate you to inflict pain on yourself; they help you escape pain.

Laughter can also trigger endorphins to release in the body. It is different from adrenaline though. Skydiving and bungee jumping trigger an adrenaline high because you anticipate pain. The adrenaline junkie is not seeking pain; he/she is seeking to avoid pain. When the brain sees lots of threat signals, it releases adrenaline.

In the past, daily life held so much physical pain that social pain was secondary. Today we spend less time suffering the pain of physical labor, predator attack, or deteriorating disease. Our attention is free to focus on pain of disappointed social expectations. This leaves us feeling life is more painful even though it is less painful than in the past.

Exercise triggers the good feeling, but the same level of exertion will soon disappoint you because you have to keep doing more to get the same feeling. If you are a person who never exercises, you will get a great release of endorphins the first day you start.

Many organizations have people doing tasks or jobs without explaining why. As we have become more of a social society, this is a huge mental trigger because explaining the why allows for employees to see the overall strategic direction and shows the value of doing certain tasks. This will allow them to make suggestions and needed improvements. We need to find a way to develop a culture which allows each employee to feel in control of his/her job.

When it comes to the workplace, most people's struggles come from process and systems, policies and procedures, and clearly defined accountability.

Chapter 5 – Keeping the Brain Healthy

Did you know that within the past 10 years researchers and scientists have learned more about the human brain than in the previous 50 years? Scientists realized through 3D imagers we can regrow parts of the brain, which was previously thought to be impossible. As we study and open our minds to new ideas, energy is driven over synapses. As we reprogram our mind, the amount of energy or force it takes to create this energy decreases because synapses create new pathways for information to travel across the brain.

The human brain is comprised of 80% water, and most humans are severely dehydrated. The human brain needs about 80-90 ounces of water per day to be considered optimally functional. Every human being needs to consider how much water he/she is drinking in order to keep the brain hydrated.

Oxygen and Glucose Supply

Glucose is the brain's sole fuel except under conditions of starvation when it breaks down protein. The brain is by far the body's hungriest organ. Although it accounts for just 2% of the body's weight, it requires a staggering 20% of our total glucose intake.

The body digests food and produces glucose to provide brain food. Think about the brain as a vital organ. If you eat high sugar foods or foods that quickly break down sugars, what happens to the brain? You will have elevated spikes in glucose which creates the highs and lows most of us experience throughout the day.

Your brain does not stop working when glucose is low. It stops doing some things and starts doing others. This may help explain why depleted people feel things more intensely than they would otherwise. Certain parts of the brain go into high gear just as other parts taper off.

Oddly enough the body uses glucose during self-control causing it to start craving sweet things to eat. This is definitely bad news for people hoping to use their self-control to avoid sweets.

NOTE: Do not skimp on calories when you are trying to deal with more serious problems than being overweight. When you need to make strategic business decisions, you want to have more glucose in your brain which comes from eating and sleeping properly. Maintain steady self-control by eating foods with a low-glycemic index: most vegetables, nuts (peanuts and cashews), many raw fruits (apples, blueberries, and pears), cheese, fish, meat, olive oil, and other good fats. Also seven to eight hours of sleep per night is critical.

Do Your Employees Have Any Of These Symptoms?

The following are warning signs of a sick organization:

1. Forgetting things (overwhelmed or stressed)
2. Low energy
3. Bad moods/talking negatively
4. Irritability or tension
5. Displaying anxiety, stress or worry
6. Short attention spans
7. Brain fog
8. Making poor decisions
9. Complaining about lack of sleep
10. Overweight

If you answered yes to most of these, it is time to rethink how you are doing things within your company. Consider doing the following:

- Get rid of the junk food in the kitchen
- Offer bottled water
- Consider offering fruit drinks instead of soda

- Encourage people to walk 30 minutes a day
- Bring in a wellness specialist to teach healthy eating
- Focus on positive instead of negative
- Encourage employees to go to the doctor for a physical

If you send your employees to the doctor, it is important to know these numbers for mental health:

1. Blood pressure
2. BMI
3. Fasting blood sugar
4. HgAIC levels
5. Vitamin D levels
6. Thyroid panel (TSH, T3, T4 antibodies)
7. Ferritin (Iron)
8. Free Total Testosterone (even for women)
9. Cortisol level

Taking Vitamin D and Fish Oil helps to increase blood flow to the brain aiding in mental clarity.

Eliminating Brain Fog

Many of our lives consist of constant stress, a poor diet, and a lack of exercise and sleep leading to what scientists call exhaustion syndrome. We know it as burnout, and it takes hold of us when we continually push through each day postponing the renewal time our body and brain needs. The mantra is "Work like crazy and then crash." This is a deadly pattern which is killing our brain capacity. It is not good for any person or organization.

As the brain gets overloaded, you begin taking on more than you can handle. As you deal with repeated interruptions, commands and conflicting demands, deep and primitive centers of the brain get activated. You get distracted, you forget, you become inefficient, and you underperform.

Many people think if they could just do more things faster, they would be more productive. Their brains are hijacked by incoming demand, and they lose the ability to discern between important and unimportant priorities. Constant interruptions not only slow down the brain but also raise stress levels.

Too much stress drains dopamine from the brain which reduces your power to think reflectively, assimilate new knowledge, and lose your creativity. According to Dr. Manfred Spitzer, "Anxious people, generally speaking, only reproduce what they already know." The human mind is programmed to turn to threats, unfinished business, failures, and unfulfilled desires when it has nothing more urgent to do and attention is left free to wander. Without a task for focusing our attention, most of us find ourselves becoming progressively depressed.

Decision Fatigue

Imagine your brain is like a fully-charged battery. When you are doing things correctly, you will wake up every morning with your battery fully charged. You have a lot of energy and you are thinking clearly. As the day progresses, your brain consumes more glucose causing the battery levels to go down. The more you have to think and strategize, the more glucose you consume. If you are not eating correctly, your battery will also lose its charge faster. If you are not drinking enough water, your battery will also go down faster. When you are forced to make tougher decisions and those factors are all in play, the result is Decision Fatigue.

As the day progresses, you go through different levels of Decision Fatigue. In the first stage, called Ego-depletion, you might be more sensitive to your emotions. Something might trigger you to be bothered or frustrated and you know you should not be. People with chronic physical pain are often people with a perpetual shortage of willpower because their minds are so depleted by the struggle to ignore the pain.

The second stage is something I refer to as the "What the Hell Effect." This is when you walk through Wal-Mart and you notice a small child begging his mother for something in a different aisle or a piece of candy. After the thirty-fifth time, the mother knows it is not the right thing to do, but she is so worn out that she breaks down, throws up her arms and says, "What the hell!" She tells the child to go get whatever it is just so long as he/she is quiet and gives her a moment's peace. Everyone has been at this stage, and everyone always lives to regret it afterward.

Changing Your Lifestyle Will Make You Perform Better

I am not a medical doctor, but the following ideas are the best practices I use. You can use these to help improve your own personal productivity:

- Since your brain is 80% water, make sure you are staying hydrated by drinking six to eight glasses of water per day.

- Take in low-glycemic carbohydrates that do not raise your blood sugar but are high in fiber.

- Think of a rainbow when eating enjoying foods of many different, natural colors. These foods are filled with antioxidants that improve your energy and help keep your brain young.

- Exercise regularly. Not only is this healthy, but exercise floods the prefrontal cortex with dopamine and allows you to think more clearly.

- Get a good night's sleep which allows your brain to process what it has learned and restructure itself around the new ideas. By contrast someone who continuously jumbles his/her natural day-and-night rhythm with artificial light, shift work, or going all night long impairs his/her memory.

- Learn to disconnect from the world. Too much stress can actually deplete our dopamine levels and release too much cortisol which can turn toxic and damage our bodies.

Chapter 6 – Stress in the Workplace

In March 2013, the National Institute of Occupational Safety & Health (NIOSH) released a study which estimated workplace stress accounted for over $300 billion in costs to United States companies. This report also showed 90% of the reasons people went to see their family physician was stress related.

That led my team and me to research what the number one stress treatment by family physicians was. The results did not add up. The number one diagnosis by family physicians was adult ADD. When I first started studying these two areas, I did not realize how closely related they were. It is very interesting that adult ADD and stress have similar signs and symptoms. Then I researched why family physicians diagnose people with adult ADD. The brain is the only organ that is treated without being examined. Many doctors do not understand how to properly treat stress. In most cases they will prescribe what I refer to as the happy pill. Unfortunately, that pill does not really treat stress; it just masks the symptoms. I was very amazed when I learned within the last ten years scientists have found natural ways the body can lower stress levels without using medicine.

I wanted to know what happens in the human body when we get stressed. I quickly learned emotions connect the body to the brain, which means we can break all our emotions down into four categories:

- Happy
- Anger
- Fear
- Sadness

When you look at these emotions, you need to understand three out of the four will trigger an emotional response which in turn triggers the release of cortisol. The release of cortisol is the human body's natural response to fight-or-flight. When cortisol is released, heart rate rises, muscles tense, and the brain goes into hyperactive mode. This causes us to become very sensitive to others around us, and we become stressed.

When you mix emotions (cortisol release) with thoughts, you can get a very dangerous response. This is what I like to refer to as an emotional cocktail. You are mixing all of those emotions into a bottle, shaking it with cortisol and pressurizing it until you are ready to blow.

As I delved more into the brain, I realized when you get to this emotional-response state, you have a part of your brain, the amygdala, which does not send normal signals to the prefrontal cortex of your brain which allows you to think normally. This almond-shaped amygdala is important to understand because it can help us recover when we get stressed.

When the amygdala is notified something is wrong, it alerts the adrenals to release cortisol which mobilizes energy by putting our entire metabolism on high alert. Cortisol is the brain's emergency broadcast system. Cortisol then is sent throughout your entire body making all your muscles tense, raising your heart rate, and affecting your thyroid and many other important organs.

A big burst of cortisol is what we call fear. Small drips of cortisol are anxiety or stress. When you feel a cortisol alert, your brain looks for a way to make it stop. The problem is most of the workforce have been having elevated levels of cortisol releases for an extended period of time or over many years. This is causing chronic illness in this country because our bodies are not prepared to handle years of elevated cortisol levels. It is no wonder people are so stressed and not as productive as they used to be.

Cortisol is also triggered by disappointment. Your brain alerts you when your expectations are not met. That "Do something!" feeling gets your attention. Bad feelings are often caused by real threats; avoiding bad feelings promotes survival. Cortisol does its job by motivating us to do what it takes to eliminate bad feelings. This response is highly adaptive in the face of short-term stress, but it can turn into a problem, with which we cannot adequately cope, triggering cortisol levels to become chronically elevated. Traumatic experiences can sensitize limbic reactivity, making it so that even minor stresses can generate cortisol to spike causing daily life to become more challenging for the traumatized person.

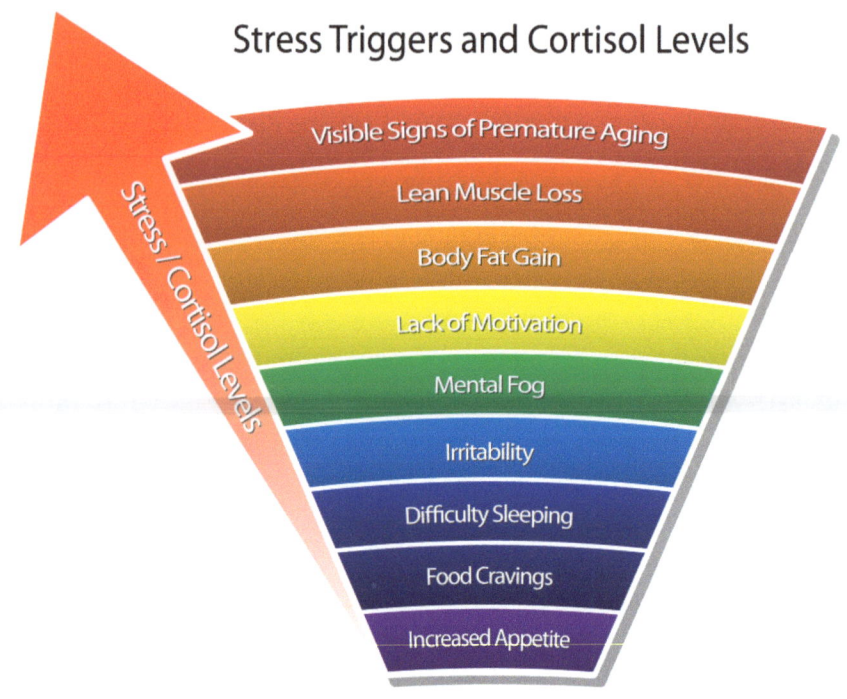

The crushing stress we live with can literally bake the brain. A stressed-out brain is continually immersed in adrenaline, a high octane chemical that overstimulates every system of the body. The result: We wear down fast, barely get through the day, and become exhausted or even ill. Eventually, we burn out.

Constant stress, poor diet, lack of exercise and sleep leads to what scientists call exhaustion syndrome. The rest of us call it burnout. We continually push through each day postponing the renewal time our bodies and brains need. The mantra is "Work like crazy and then crash." Furthermore, we get rewarded for the ordinary mindset; it becomes a badge of honor to brag about being up until midnight or working through the whole weekend. Someone suggests vacation, and we think they are crazy and not a go-getter. Sadly this pattern is killing our brain capacity and is no good for the organization either.

We live in a high-pressure environment. It is exhilarating at times but also taxing on our energy, draining it away rapidly. A certain amount of stress is actually energizing; however, if the stress goes on too long, it can turn toxic and damage our bodies and brains.

It is comforting to know bad feelings have a purpose, but it is not complimentary to the old style of management which is triggered by fear or intimidation. I have noticed most of my students have negative responses to this type of management style because they become overly sensitive to stress resulting in most of them beginning to shut down.

Another great supplement to lower stress is maca, a root vegetable related to the turnip and grown in the mineral-rich volcanic soil of the Peruvian highlands. Maca possesses the building blocks or precursors for serotonin. The body will often try to self-medicate when it is feeling overwhelmed by stress-induced chemical reactions in the brain. It is at this time sugar cravings, the brain's attempt to raise serotonin levels, are prevalent. A diet which includes a daily dose of maca will supply the body with what it needs to help curtail stress and construct serotonin.

Old World Leadership Style – Push

The management style of the past was designed around the Industrial Revolution era. It was very well suited for that time frame because it allowed people to have a very heretical structure much like today's military. The top person was in charge; if you bucked the system, you paid the price. I can recall seeing it firsthand when I was younger: I went to work with my dad occasionally and heard him talking to his secretary just as he would talk to one of his children. His tone was very harsh, and he would hand over a stack of papers saying he needed the reports completed by 4:00 P.M. the following day. Then he walked away. There was never a please or thank you.

The old world of management style is geared to basically tell people what to do and expect them to do it. If they did not like what you told them or how you told them, tough. People were not paid to be happy; they merely worked to get paid. Well, thankfully those days are almost gone.

When I am doing a presentation in front of a group, I often demonstrate this activity for them:

> I call someone to the front of the room and ask him/her to stand next to me. Then I ask him/her to count the steps as we walk toward a particular object. Once I know he/she is walking next to me, I ask him/her to count the steps out loud with me. Once we get to the object, I ask him/her to stop and tell the group how many paces he/she took.
>
> Next, I will go back to the starting point and have the person come back half way. He/she is instructed to put up his/her hands and face me. I say, "I am going to put my hands on yours, and I am going to push you back to the spot we paced off." He/she nods, showing he/she understands. I then get in an almost football-type stance and ask if he/she has any questions before we begin. I begin to push and guess what? Almost every person pushes back. He/she acknowledges he/she knows the rules: I was going to push him/her to the spot we marked out. Still he/she resists. The logical question is "Why?" The answer is simple: People do not like to be pushed.
>
> Afterward, I will walk back to the beginning spot and motion with my finger for him/her to come toward me. Everyone always comes and stands next to me. I do not even speak a word.

The remaining question: How are we going to manage this next generation of workers if we have a high-stress workplace and they all begin shutting down?

Leading with Influence

Leading with influence is so much harder, but it is critical because you need to get people involved. Include the team in the decision-making process, and find out what motivates them. Most people do not want to do this for one main reason: It takes too much time. However, in today's world you have to do this. People are raised differently. They go to schools where everything is done in teams with nobody winning or losing. Everyone gets to participate; everyone gets to give his/her opinions. This is something we have created, and it is becoming a part of human nature we must acknowledge and address in business.

When it comes to running a business, we have to set these boundaries in play for people to feel a part of something bigger than themselves. They have to feel part of the team. I have found that everyone must have clear goals within their job and adequate feedback to make this happen. Creating a common link to the overall purpose of their job and how it impacts the overall vision of the company is critical.

Influence is really about getting people to understand and seeing things the way you see them. When it comes to influencing an organization or another person, ask yourself the following questions:

- What do I need to teach him/her about his/her way of thinking about something?
- How can I get him/her to see this issue the same way I see it?
- What information or data do I have to help guide me in this?

When you are able to do this unconsciously, you have become someone who has great influence on others.

Chapter 7 – Results Based Economy

September 11, 2001, started a downward spiral that has impacted us in so many ways. Then in 2008, we experienced another downward trend in the economy referred to as the Great Recession. This recession was a longer length of time in years than what many people experienced in the Great Depression. I love talking about this in my economics classes because when you look at and study history, it tells us so much about what to expect in the future. If you look at the Great Depression, you can tell this was a very difficult time for so many people.

I remember as a very small child walking into my grandmother's house. My grandma lived in a very small house (approximately 1500 square feet) in a St. Louis suburb. It was always special to go see Grandma, but it was a real treat when we did visit and she asked us to do something that took us into a room or area of her house which we were not always allowed. During one visit I was asked to go into the dining room (I must say that in all my years I never ate a meal in her dining room.) and go to the door that led to the attic. In many of the houses in her subdivision, there was a door somewhere inside the house that led to an attic. My dad talks about his room being upstairs, but I cannot even imagine living in such a cold, dark place. I remember this so vividly because the right side of the staircase held stacks and stacks of newspapers. I remember once asking my grandmother why she saved every newspaper. Her answer was one I will always remember:

"Matt, you have no idea what newspapers can do for you. You can line your clothes, place it in your bed to keep you warm, or use it to clean your windows."

Of course being a little child and not knowing anything, I often said, "Why would you just not turn up the heat or put on another blanket if you were cold?" My grandma often said in laughter if I was ever cold, I would understand. I would watch my dad roll his eyes and think how silly she was, but what I never realized was that she had lived through the Great Depression. She went through so many days, weeks and even months without food and warmth. It was not until I was much older and studying the impacts of the Great Depression that I even began to comprehend what my grandmother was talking about.

What has this done to our workplaces? It has created a great deal of workplace stress and impacted all of our jobs. It has literally closed businesses and has broken people who cannot cope with changes. We have made a major shift from trading time for money to a result-based economy. A result-based economy is one in which people expect to see results instead of complaining. Our society is so pressured to produce results that when you hear an excuse of why something cannot be done, you do not really listen. All you want to hear is how much you have accomplished. This is our new economy.

A Results Based Economy

Time & Effort Jobs

- Job Security
- Guaranteed Income
- Routine
- Limited Control Of Your Future
- Standardized Jobs
- Uniformity
- Conformity
- Bureaucratic

Results Based Jobs

- High Level of Income
- Results Provided
- Complete Accountability
- Value Adding
- Quality Driven
- Relationship Intensive
- Innovative
- Customizable

OLD WORLD MANAGEMENT STYLE

INFLUENCE BASED

VALLEY OF RISK

The High Performance Business Model

As you can see from the graphic, we are a result-based economy. Why are so many American companies not able to thrive? I started to reflect this as a teacher, business owner and someone studying what was going on with major businesses and why some companies were able to succeed and others were not so lucky.

Complete Accountability

I noticed something which I believe is the missing link in many businesses today. Many business owners develop a very comprehensive business plan and a distribution system. They spend much time understanding marketing, but they never teach a real business model to the workforce. Let me define a business model for you as every leader or supervisor operates under a certain model. Whether you are in Human Resources, Marketing or Sales, you must all operate within these defined terms. Most people expect every leader to know how to operate, but the fact of the matter is he/she does not. He/she does not really know how to hold everyone to the same standards. Because of this I developed The High Performance Business Model to give guidelines about how to operate each business unit. Remember: this business model operates under the umbrella of The High Achievers Framework. If you want to learn more about this, read my book The High Performance Business Model.

The High Performance Business Model

Creating a business model which works well for many types of organizations and is easy to understand was necessary for me to begin my outreach to the growing number of organizations looking for a new way to work – one that focused on the overall quality of work combined with the organizations' goals and results.

In order to achieve a healthy, productive, and happy workplace you must

Provide clear goals.
Provide adequate feedback.
Provide a balance of skills *vs.* abilities.
Make employees feel connected.
Never devalue an employee's time.

The High Performance Business Model looks similar to the organizational model, but it is focused on the areas of Energy, Connections, Influence, and Integration.

The process below was developed to see where organizations fall into our model:

Business Analysis

High Achievers
Leadership Training

Company Name: _____ Date: _____

Please rank each statement below on a scale of 1 to 5 with 1 as the weakest and 5 as the strongest.

Energy	1	2	3	4	5
1. We have a clear mission in writing that has been properly communicated and is shared by everyone.					
2. Everyone has goals and is focused on them.					
3. Everyone is engaged in regular weekly meetings and we review progress.					
4. We have a current method of measuring our progress that is easily available to everyone.					
5. Our yearly goals are clear and have been communicated to everyone.					
Total					

Connections		1	2	3	4	5
1.	Our purpose is clear, and we are hiring, reviewing, rewarding and firing around our purpose.					
2.	Our core business is clear and our systems and processes reflect that.					
3.	My immediate Supervisor is the right person for the job.					
4.	The people I supervise are the right people for the job.					
5.	Those I supervise are open, honest and demonstrate a high level of trust.					
	Total					

Influence		1	2	3	4	5
1.	My immediate Supervisor is empowering and leads with the best interests of the organization in mind.					
2.	Those that I supervise perform their day-to-day activities with the best interests of the organization in mind.					
3.	Our accountability chart (organizational chart of roles and responsibilities) is clear and complete.					
4.	My immediate Supervisor is open, honest and demonstrates a high level of trust.					
5.	All teams clearly identify, discuss, and solve key issues for the greater good and long term progress.					
	Total					

Integration		1	2	3	4	5
1.	We have a budget and are monitoring per business unit, and the Leader has control.					
2.	There is a system in place for receiving regular employee feedback, and issues are addressed in an appropriate amount of time.					
3.	Our systems and processes are documented, simplified, and followed by all.					
4.	All meetings have a printed agenda, a clear start and end time as well as a clearly defined purpose.					
5.	We have a proven process for doing business with our clients. It has been named and visually illustrated, and everyone is adhering to it.	.				
	Total					

Score Results	1	2	3	4	5
Total number of each from the sub-groups					
Multiply each by	X1	X2	X3	X4	X5
Total for each column					
Add all five numbers to determine the percentage score that reflects the current state of your Company.					

If your score falls between

100% - 91:   High Performance

90% - 80:   Innovation

79% - 65:   Engagement

64% - 50:   Courage

49% - 35:   Frustration

34% - 21:   Worry

20% - Below: Apathy

Filling out the Business Analysis at least twice per year will clarify all gaps, put those issues into action, and ultimately enable you to continue to climb toward 100%. The goal is progress, not perfection. You might feel frustrated that your score is not as high as you would like it to be. Yet success is not based on where you are but on how far you have come. If you were at 55% last year and 63% this year, that is success. The next year you may reach 72%, and if you are committed, that percentage will keep climbing higher.

Chapter 8 - Conclusion

As I have gone down this journey, I have realized so many things I want other people to know and understand. I want people to understand that while working within an organization, we can purposefully do things to make our employees more engaged and happier.

What is fascinating to me is the human mind is programmed to turn to threats, unfinished business, failures, and worst-case scenarios when it has nothing more urgent to do. It wanders to places that are not helpful for a happier life. No wonder so many people are getting depressed. This fact, along with jobs to which they do not attach a perceived value, means people cannot connect themselves to a bigger purpose.

Organizations must provide the following in the workplace:

- Clear goals.
- Adequate feedback.
- Challenges for its people – a balance of skills vs. knowledge.
- A sense of control for employees.
- Appropriate use of time for employees.

To achieve this every manager and leader must invest a great deal of mental energy into monitoring and enhancing the well-being of the entire group. The group MUST develop self-discipline in order to focus on individual self-awareness and not act selfishly. Whenever a leader cuts corners, shows favoritism, or is unfair or thoughtless, he/she undermines the common interest of the group.

Creating the High Achievers Framework has been an awesome experience. I have been able to find a way to take the old school leadership style of push and convert to the new leadership style of influence.

Understanding this model will provide you the tools to design a culture of continuously happy people. You need to remember the following:

Energy releases dopamine which is important for everyone to feel good and have more energy. You can release dopamine by

- Tying every employee's job back to the organization's mission, vision, and values.
- Including every employee in setting clear goals with frequent reward systems.
- Updating people weekly (similar to a computer game).
- Developing performance measures as a means for the employees to know if they are winning or losing in their own job.
- Providing a purpose-driven schedule so time is not wasted.
- Holding employees accountable to the core values of the organization.
- Including employees in the hiring process when you need to add people to your team.
- Finding employees doing things right and telling them. They will continue to do things to earn positive recognition.

Connections release oxytocin which promotes bonding. This is important because it helps the processing of social cues involved in the recognition of individuals. It is also referred to as the trust hormone because the human body can sense when it trusts someone. The release of oxytocin is also somewhat addictive. The other side benefit is that it is the body's natural defense mechanism against cortisol. You can literally reach up into your brain and release oxytocin by giving people hugs, doing sincere things to help others, and just telling them thank you. You can release oxytocin by

- Explaining the overall company goals and history and connecting how the employee's job correlates to the goals of the organization.

- Having frequent meetings with your employee to ask where he/she wants to be in his/her career.

- Including the employee in the hiring process so he/she has input about with whom he/she will work in order to bond.

- Creating a transparent organization.

- Building an atmosphere that is open and with free-flowing communication; one that does not allow others to talk about each other behind people's backs.

- Forcing your managers to grow every employee.

- Pushing every employee to learn new skills and then having he/she apply them at work.

- Understanding all team members' communication styles.

- Focusing on internal customers as much as external customers.

- Focusing on the group, not just a select few.

- Creating teamwork, not silos.

Influence releases serotonin, the chemical your family physician prescribes in the anxiety or happy pill. Serotonin is important because it is linked to love and pride of being a part of something. It makes us feel good. You can increase serotonin by

- Empowering people to complete tasks and develop new ways of doing things but holding them accountable.
- Developing systems of complete accountability to let every employee know if he/she is winning or losing in his/her job.
- Publicly displaying organizational charts with levels of authority and decision making.
- Continually building and restoring trust.
- Making decisions that are beneficial to the organization, not individuals.
- Showing equality, not favoritism.
- Learning to delegate effectively. Do not just hand someone a project.
- Identifying and rewarding positive behaviors.
- Including everyone in scheduling challenges.
- Realizing customer service is internal as well as external.
- Conducting open, honest performance evaluation systems.
- Acknowledging leadership needs are held accountable.

Integration equals endorphins. It has been proven over and over the closer you get to a goal, the harder you work. In my organization we have a lot of very small goals. When people get close, they will do extraordinary things to make sure they complete even the smallest of goals. Then we reward them. Endorphins allow you to push through pain. If you continue, you will reach the state of euphoria, that good feeling of which you cannot get enough. You can increase endorphins by

- Having clearly defined processes.

- Tying all meetings to business objectives and conducting them with an agenda and accountability.

- Monitoring and tracking the budget and communicating it to everyone.

- Ensuring everyone knows performance goals and KPIs and where he/she stands.

- Making sure employee issues are addressed in a timely manner and dealt with properly.

- Continually evaluating and updating processes/systems.

- Empowering others to cross train.

- Ensuring reports are written correctly and all information is being communicated.

- Having systems to organize workflow.

- Following through.

I want to leave you with the understanding that there is much more within your control to create a happy, healthy organization. Understanding positive intelligence is critical to make this happen because we can reprogram the brain to think and act positively. We are learning that people who can take a negative subject and find the good are much healthier, happier, and better leaders. Organizations will benefit from this.

I hope you will explore making your organization Working Happy.

Appendix

Organization Happiness

Integration = Endorphins	Energy = Dopamine
○ Have clearly defined processes. ○ Tie meetings to goals/objectives. ○ Monitor and communicate the budget. ○ Communicate and track Business Unit KPIs. ○ Address issues in a timely manner. ○ Update processes and accountability as needed. ○ Support ongoing training both personally and professionally. ○ Empower others to cross training. ○ Ensure reports are written correctly and information is communicated to all parties. ○ Organize work flow. ○ Have clear accountability. ○ Follow through.	○ Understanding the overall job of the employee and how it ties back to the organization. ○ Making sure the employee understands the mission and vision of the organization, helping he/she realize he/she is tied to something bigger than himself/herself. ○ Including the employee in setting team goals as well as his/her own goals. ○ Making sure employees and leaders frequently communicate the organizational goals. ○ Providing frequent progress meetings as to how he/she is doing. ○ Developing performance measures and business unit KPIs to let the employee know if he/she is winning or losing at his/her job. ○ Providing a purpose-driven schedule. ○ Making sure employee understands the core values of the organization and holding him/her accountable. ○ Including him/her in hiring new employees. ○ Evaluating performance frequently.

Influence = Serotonin	Connections = Oxytocin
○ Empower workers to complete tasks and also hold them accountable. ○ Develop systems for complete accountability (see The High Performance Business Model). ○ Have public organizational charts with decision-level responsibilities identified. ○ Continually build and work on restoring and/or maintaining trust. ○ Make decisions based on the good of the organization and not just a select few. ○ Learn how to effectively delegate. ○ Remove barriers to success. ○ Identify positive behaviors and reward those behaviors. ○ Include the group in scheduling. ○ Realize that customer service is not a one-size-fits-all model. ○ Conduct honest, open performance evaluations. ○ Make sure leaders are conducting their accountability checkups at the time and date set. ○ Inspect what you expect.	○ Explaining the overall organizational purpose and how the employee's job relates to the purpose starts to build a connection. ○ Including employees in the hiring process and allowing them to help determine who is a good fit for an organization builds a connection and trust. ○ Organizations that are transparent and do not hide things from employees are more connected. ○ Building an atmosphere so employees can have open communications. ○ Leaders focusing on developing and growing employees will connect them to the organization. ○ Employees need to be encouraged in a positive direction in relation to job skills vs. knowledge. ○ Understanding team members' communication styles is important. ○ Organizations need to focus on internal customer service as much as external customer service. ○ Leaders need to teach people to develop, grow, and take risks. ○ Leaders disseminate information to all employees, not just a select few. ○ Leaders motivate and create a sense of teamwork through teambuilding and working through issues.

Employee Happiness

Integration = Endorphins	Energy = Dopamine
○ Exercise three-four times a week. ○ Develop process and procedures for clearly defined accountability. ○ Push yourself to become better. ○ Promote yourself in the workplace. ○ Experience healthy pain. ○ Work within your life's mission. ○ Allow yourself to fail and learn from your mistakes. ○ Look towards the future and envision something better. ○ Practice delayed gratification. ○ Meet others and share your story.	○ Set goals (small, medium, and large as well as personal and professional). ○ Work in areas of inner strengths. ○ Work within boundaries for a balance of fun. ○ Communicate effectively with others. ○ Understand positive intelligence. ○ Meditate. ○ Stay active with health & fitness (floods prefrontal cortex with dopamine to clear mind). ○ Develop a clear-accountability plan. ○ Know if you are winning or losing at any moment. ○ Balance work/life (time management). ○ Develop internal rewards for your job.

Influence = Serotonin	Connections = Oxytocin
<ul><li>Show respect to others.</li><li>Respect yourself.</li><li>Plan ninety days out for your job.</li><li>Identify inner strengths and work within them.</li><li>Work within your life mission</li><li>Promote workplace stability</li><li>Minimize workplace conflict.</li><li>Build long-term relationships</li><li>Allow yourself to forgive.</li><li>Believe in a higher spiritual being.</li><li>Make the workplace fun and laugh frequently.</li><li>Inspect what you expect.</li></ul>	<ul><li>Only take jobs that you feel you can make a difference.</li><li>Become "connected" to co-workers.</li><li>Value close friendships.</li><li>Maintain healthy two-sided family relationships.</li><li>Find someone with whom you can share your thoughts and feelings.</li><li>Perform at least three sincere acts of kindness for others weekly.</li><li>Tell others "Thank you" frequently.</li><li>Attend one networking event monthly.</li><li>Get involved within your community.</li><li>Become part of a team/group.</li><li>Respond to emails/voicemails daily.</li></ul>

Individual Happiness

Integration = Endorphins	Energy = Dopamine
○ Exercise and push yourself. ○ Have processes or routines to simplify life. ○ Push yourself to become better. ○ Promote yourself. ○ Allow yourself to experience healthy pain. ○ Have a life mission/purpose. ○ Allow yourself to fail and learn from your mistakes. ○ Look towards the future and envision something better. ○ Understand delayed gratification. ○ Read/learn new skills.	○ Set Goals ○ Work in areas of inner strengths. ○ Spend time having fun. ○ Practice effective communication. ○ Use positive intelligence. ○ Meditate/mindful techniques. ○ Exercise (floods prefrontal cortex with dopamine to clear mind). ○ Follow your dreams. ○ Stay out of debt. ○ Balance work/life (time management). ○ Play games with rewards.

Influence = Serotonin	**Connections = Oxytocin**
○ Show respect for others. ○ Show respect for yourself. ○ Plan for the future. ○ Know your strengths. ○ Have a clear vision for your life. ○ Promote stability. ○ Minimize conflict. ○ Build relationships. ○ Learn to forgive. ○ Have a spiritual belief. ○ Have fun and laugh. ○ Inspect what you expect.	○ Be part of something bigger than yourself. ○ Become connected to co-workers. ○ Value friendships. ○ Spend quality time with family. ○ Share your dreams and passions with others ○ Do sincere acts of kindness. ○ Tell people "Thank you." ○ Meet new people. ○ Get involved in your community. ○ Belong to groups/teams. ○ Respond to emails/voicemails with enthusiasm. ○ Hug people and smile every day.

The following "**High Achievers Leadership Tools**" were developed to give leaders or those wanting to gain leadership skills current, practical, cutting edge tools and methodologies that they can take back to their work place and use the very next day.

Integration = Endorphins	Energy = Dopamine
○ The Pinnacle Path™ ○ Your Learning Experience™ ○ The Opportunity Analysis™ ○ Your Frustration Breakthrough™ ○ The Accountability Finder™ ○ The Business Opportunity Finder™ ○ Your Project Roadmap™ ○ Your Compass Analyzer™ ○ The High Achievers Navigator™	○ The 90 Day Target™ ○ Delegation Navigator™ ○ Your Meeting Planner™ ○ My Weekly Planner™ ○ The Daily Dashboard™ ○ The Leadership Time Solution™ ○ Your Strategic Vision™
Influence = Serotonin	**Connections = Oxytocin**
○ Social Conflict Model™ ○ The Dimension Model™ ○ The Trust Model™ ○ Generational Conflict Model™ ○ The Yearly Target™ ○ Your Hiring Filter™ ○ You vs. Role™ ○ TAIS Assessment	○ Social Conflict Model™ ○ The Dimension Model™ ○ The Communicator™ ○ Extended DISC® ○ The High Performance Playbook™ ○ My Weekly Planner™ ○ Evaluating Performance™ ○ The Experience Finder™

Ascend Business Strategies offers executive coaching and consulting services focusing on employee engagement, personal effectiveness, leadership, and change management. From conflict resolution to goal setting, we not only provide live training but also send our participants home with sustainable models they can use again and again. You will gain competencies through the following course segments:

- Foundation: Your Brain and The Workplace
- Your Hiring Filter™
- The Delegation Navigator™
- My Weekly Planner™
- The Pinnacle Path™ (Problem Solving/Goal Setting)
- The Dimension Model™ (Conflict Resolution)
- Your Meeting Planner™
- Bonus: Your Learning Experience™

If you are not as passionate about your work or home life as you have been in the past, if your energy level and connections are not as vibrant and alive as they have been, if you would like your influence level in your professional and/or personal life to be more lasting and impactful, or maybe you simply want to have greater results from the efforts you put forth on a daily basis, we can help.

For more information:

www.highachieversleadership.com

Whether you are an aspiring leader or want to refine your leadership skills, High Achievers Leadership Training is the course for you. This one-day course covers the imperatives of successful leadership. From planning and hiring to conflict resolution and goal setting, you will walk away with incredible insights and the tools to put these important concepts into practice.

www.successinhiring.com

What keeps successful organizations on top? Surveys show specific hiring practices and tools are directly linked to an organization's success. Effective hiring systems have ranked higher in financial performance, productivity, quality, customer satisfaction, employee satisfaction and retention. We feel success is based on finding the right people for the right job. This course will provide you with the tools you need to have for success in hiring.

www.matthewcowell.com

The High Achievers Framework will help you utilize your wisdom by reflecting on your experiences and the knowledge that helped you get to this point professionally and personally. You will use that experience to create clarity for your business and personal life. You will establish what new habits and disciplines you need to do in order to move forward on your journey. The High Achievers Framework demonstrates how ENERGY + CONNECTIONS + INFLUENCE + INTEGRATION = GREATER RESULTS for your company and your own personal life.

NOTES AND REFERENCES

Daniel Amen (2012). Use Your Brain To Change Your Age. Secrets to look, feel, and think younger every day.

David DiSalvo (2011). What makes your brain happy and why you should do the opposite?

Mihaly Csikszentmihalyi (1990). Flow, the psychology of optimal Experience. "Important….. Illuminates the way to happiness.

Mihaly Csikszentmihalyi (2003). Good Business. Leadership, Flow, and the making of meaning.

David R. Hawkins, M.D., Ph.D. (2012). Power vs. Force. The Hidden Determinants of Human Behavior.

David R. Hawkins, M.D., Ph.D. (2006). Transcending The Levels of Consciousness. The Stairway To Enlightenment.

Loretta Grazian Bruening, Ph.D (2012). Meet Your Happy Chemicals.

To learn more or for a free consultation, contact us

Ascend Business Strategies

www.ascendbusinessstrategies.com

or call 1-866-549-0434

www.ingramcontent.com/pod-product-compliance
Lightning Source LLC
Chambersburg PA
CBHW040833180526
45159CB00001B/179